The Book o:
and Divining

by Sue Phillips

with illustrations by Morgan Phillips

The Book of Dowsing and Divining

©2000 Sue Phillips

ISBN 186163 1200

Internal illustrations by Morgan Phillips
Cover design by Paul Mason

Published by:

Capall Bann Publishing
Freshfields
Chieveley
Berks
RG20 8TF

Dedication

This book is dedicated with love to my daughter Marianne
Phillips who helped me perfect my dowsing technique
over the past few years, and has helped and encouraged
me when things got tough.

Acknowledgements

I would like to thank all those people who have allowed me the privilege of dowsing them over the years and the landowners on whose property I have dowsed - especially my parents whose love and support means so much to me, and my son Jonathan, who modelled for many of the dowsing photographs at extremely short notice.

I would also like to thank Anna Franklin for teaching me the basics of pendulum dowsing amongst so many other things. Many of the psychic insulation techniques detailed in this book were first shown to me by Anna, who also first introduced me to the existence of the chakras.

Finally, of course I would like to thank my family for their encouragement, patience, and forbearance during the writing of this little book.

My thanks to all.

Other Capall Bann books by the same author

Pagan Feasts with Anna Franklin (1997)
Healing Stones (1998)

4

Contents

Introduction

It's funny how the most valuable knowledge can arrive in seemingly meaningless fragments that don't actually come together for many years.

The first time I heard the term dowsing, I thought it had to do with putting out a fire, or throwing a bucket of water over somebody. I heard of divining quite early in my life but it was many years before I discovered that dowsing and divining are two different words with the same basic meaning - a method of picking up information that is hidden from view.

Most people have seen or heard of water diviners. I have an early childhood memory of watching a man striding purposely across a meadow holding a forked stick in a most peculiar way. Suddenly, the end of the stick twitched and dipped. He stopped and announced that he had found the source of an underground stream and that the farmer who had employed him should sink a well at just that spot. There seemed no doubt about his accuracy. He had the power to find water and would, in the fullness of time be proven correct. The well was sunk and commenced to supply the required water.

I was enthralled. To see magic at first hand was exciting for a six year old and I was completely in awe of the powers of that mysterious water diviner. I never saw that magical man again and in the way of many children, the event slipped from my immediate memory as my days filled with other things.

When I was ten I became a regular viewer of a daily current affairs television programme that followed Children's teatime television. My favourite part of the show was a section devoted to people with weird and wacky talents. Some people were strange, others downright peculiar. I watched a renowned 'psychic' drive a car blindfold down a busy street. He crashed within the first ten yards and was arrested, on air, for dangerous driving. Another day a man proved the phenomenal strength of his lungs by blowing up a rubber hot water bottle until it burst. There was a man whose hobby was putting half a dozen live ferrets into his trousers (or pants if you are American). He sat, straight faced as the fabric heaved around his legs, mentioning at frequent intervals that he had just been bitten.

One day they invited on a fellow who claimed to be able to find water by using bent welding rods. The test consisted of half a dozen identical containers, all covered. Five were empty, the sixth had water in, and it was his job to locate it. He picked up his rods, bent into 'L' shapes, and held them out in front of him over each container in turn. The rods remained parallel over the first two containers, but when he moved on to the third, they crossed over as if by magic. Here, he said, was the water. He was right. The buckets were shuffled round and the test done several times more, with the same success. The man insisted that he had no special powers. The welding rods would work for anyone who cared to try. The interviewer had a go, and succeeded, so my family and I hurried outside to try the experiment for ourselves. My father had a welding machine, so welding rods were easy to come by. We

8

played the new game enthusiastically and were as successful as the man on the television had predicted. I could do magic - my whole family could do magic!

Wow!

Our farm was connected to the water mains and streams and brooks trickled along at least one side of every field, so the practical benefits of our new-found talent were not immediately obvious and dowsing was again forgotten for many years.

When I grew up and started a family, I was introduced to a test to determine the sex of an unborn child by suspending a sewing needle by its thread and holding this over the 'bump' in my tummy. It was supposed to swing back and forth for a boy, or round in a circle for a girl. Well, it swung round in a circle and I had a boy. We tried the same technique on my second pregnancy and it swung to and fro, the sign for a boy. I had a girl. A few years later, I fell pregnant again. Some-body I knew said that the only reliable test was to tie a single hair to a wedding ring and use this. The swing indicated a boy, but sceptical by this time, I just laughed. This was clearly an old wives' tale to be scoffed at. I had a girl.

There was a pattern there, but I hadn't the brains to see it. Had I gone on to have another three or four children, it might have become obvious that rather than the test being consistently wrong, I was consistently misreading the result! I now know that the pendulum swing is not standard but varies a little for everyone.

Chapter 1

Dowsing Is Rather Like Riding a Bike - Easy Once You Can Do It!

The traditional diviner walks across a field with a forked hazel twig, also known as a twitch, grasped between his two hands. When he gets near to underground water courses it starts to twitch, either pointing up, or down and sometimes twisting completely round and threatening to poke him in the face if he is holding the twitch too closely. What is less obvious to the casual observer, though, is that the hazel twitch is the instrument of the diviner (or dowser). It does not have any specific powers of its own. Hazel is used for its flexibility and growth form, which gives forked branches of equal thickness - one for each hand. It could just as easily be a piece of green elder or willow of suitable shape and size. Some diviners even use strips of whalebone or plastic tied together at one end.

Dowsing can also be done using other tools, including a pendulum or a pair of metal rods bent into 'L' shapes as I and my family did all those years ago. It doesn't seem to matter what kind of metal the rods are made from, different dowsers have their own favourites. The dowser holds one in each hand loosely in a way reminiscent of a gunfighter with both guns drawn. When water or any other substance being dowsed for is located, the rods cross over. One might say 'X' marks the spot with this method and it is popular for outdoor use where strong winds might make a pendulum uncontrollable.

There are two different basic forms of dowsing. The first is passive - the use of a pendulum, dowsing rods or hazel twitch to gain information about the world around us usually locked up in the subconscious part of the brain, generally believed to be the seat of intuition. The second is active - the use of a dowsing medium - usually a pendulum, to actually have a magical effect. This is usually done in healing to affect the activity of energy centres within the body, also known as chakras. For the purpose of simple diagnosis, pendulum dowsing is by far the most practical. It has the advantage of being both very portable (try putting a forked stick in your pocket) and relatively safe - a pendulum can swing fairly strongly in the hands of an experienced dowser, but it tends to be easier to dodge than something more rigid.

Once you can dowse, you will find it possible to detect all sorts of things, from underground watercourses and buried treasure to health imbalances!

The Tools
As we've already learned, dowsing can be done with a variety of tools, depending on the circumstances, and on the preferences of the dowser. Most can be bought nowadays, but can equally easily be made. I find that home made devices tend to be better to work with as you put a little of yourself into the making.

Chapter 2

Diviner's Twitch, Or Forked Twig

Forked divining twigs are extremely simple to make and, in common with other dowsing media, can be made from any suitable material. Shaped metal, whalebone and plastic have all been used by dowsers, but traditionally, thin, forked branches are cut or snapped from ash, hazel, rowan, or willow trees. Often after high winds, it is possible to find thin branches on the ground around trees that can be used. It is best to get a branch with forks of equal thickness. Uneven branches are useable, but tricky.

The thickness is relevant. If too thick, the tool will not be responsive, if too thin, it will not last very long. This is where you need to use your judgement as your own strength will be the deciding factor.

Generally, it is possible to determine the probable flexibility of the wood by the species of tree it came from. The traditional sources provide flexible wood with no thorns, an important consideration. They also provide reasonably symmetrical forks, which is helpful. Some trees provide apparently ideally symmetrical forks, but the wood is too brittle and will snap with repeated use. Others, like conifers, tend to be rather too soft and the wood of thin branches can be covered in a rough bark that is not particularly easy to remove.

The traditional woods also have occult significance which might influence the dowser's choice, but to be honest, for most practical purposes, these are irrelevant. You can even use freshly cut brittle woods, so long as you only intend to use them once or twice before they harden.

Near to my house is a small stream, fringed with a variety of trees where children play. Often twigs get snapped and trodden underfoot. Once I found a green elder branch on the ground. It had the look of a rather leafy divining rod about it, so I picked it up and held it in the prescribed manner. It soon began to perform, twisting around so enthusiastically it almost put my eye out as I came close to running water. If you decide to copy my experiment, remember that elder is toxic, so wash your hands afterwards.

To Make a Forked Divining Twig

Materials and equipment:

* Forked branch of suitable thickness and flexibility so that when the forks are pushed outwards, there is resistance, but no danger of snapping. The forks should be as symmetrical as possible

* Knife, hacksaw or strong secuteurs

  1. Cut the single stem about six to eight inches from the joint.

13

14

2. Cut the forked stems to equal lengths slightly less than the length of your arms from shoulder to wrist. The twig may well rotate in a full circle in use, so be careful not to leave the tines too long.

3. To test take hold of either end of the forked branches, keeping the joint furthest away from you. Bend the branches out away from each other. You should feel some resistance, but it should not cause discomfort when you hold it for a few minutes, neither should it seem in danger of snapping or splitting. If it feels right, it probably is.

4. Remove the bark if preferred. The bark may be left on, though it can be rough against the skin, so a good compromise is to remove the bark from the handle portions.

Dowsing With a Forked Twig

The Grip
There is a particular method of gripping a forked twig for divining. Its one of those things that are very difficult to describe, yet easy to do. The main aim is to put the wood under stress, so that it will react to the slightest movement of the dowser's hands.

* Place each hand on either forked branch with the palms facing and your fingers and thumb wrapped securely around the branch.

* In a fluid movement, still gripping the branches, twist your hands over until your thumbs face away from each other - as if you were looking at the underside of your fists.

* Keep your arms out in front of you about waist height
  and slightly flexed. The joint where the branches meet
  should be in front and pointed away from you, far
  enough so that the tip can safely twist round full circle
  without touching you. If you cannot comfortably
  stretch your arms far enough forward for this to
  happen, the twitch is too big and must either be
  shortened, or a smaller one made.

If you find you prefer to hold your dowsing twig another
way, do so by all means. There are no hard and fast
rules.

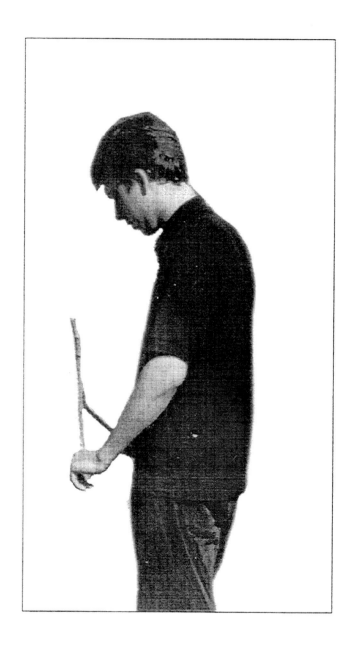

18

The Technique

This method is generally employed out of doors as it is not particularly affected by the weather and the movement of the twig can tend to be rather strong, which could break a few plates in a china shop.

Decide what it is you are searching for, whether a water course - the commonest use for such a device - or for buried treasure or archaeological evidence. If you have never dowsed before, it might be useful to perform a few control experiments first so that you will understand the signals when they come.

Looking for water is the easiest, so holding your forked twig, walk towards a stream or pond you know about. As you approach, the end should begin to dip or rise - either can be equally correct.

In a lot of cases, the nearer you get, the more active it becomes. Be careful to hold it well away from your face, it will hurt if it hits you (sorry I keep going on about this, but it does hurt when it happens). Sometimes, the whole thing twists round in a complete circle when water is directly beneath it. For some people it quivers and dips, pointing towards the water. Make a note of the way it works for you.

Repeat the experiment a few times until you are confident, then try some different materials - iron is a good one. Ask a friend to hide a large nail or something else made of iron in your garden and use your forked divining stick to try to find it. Concentrate on the material you are searching for. Some people have trouble with this, so handle the item before it is hidden and get a really good feel for it, or sometime even hold an item made of the same substance. This is called a witness.

Be prepared to find more than the single item that has been hidden - things get lost in gardens. Remember, practice makes perfect, so carry on with different materials for as long as your friend's patience lasts - it helps if they are interested in learning as well, you can take it in turns to 'hide the thimble'.

By the end you might well have found all kinds of things that people have lost through the years - you never know - there might even be some buried treasure there!

When you feel confident, you can move onto useful things, like underground water courses. Use the same technique, concentrating on finding water and see if you can map out the course of underground water pipes leading through your land. You can always check this later on plans.

When you've done all that successfully, award yourself a pat on the back and plan your first dowsing adventure.

Remember that you cannot dowse on somebody else's land without permission and that different countries have their own laws regarding ownership of what is found - please stay within the law of the land you are in.

Chapter 3
Dowsing Rods

My first dowsing experiences were with bent metal rods, and these are still very popular. Shops near to ancient sacred sites often sell sets to visitors, but they are so easy to make, it seems hardly worth the bother.

To Make a Set of Dowsing Rods

Materials and equipment:

* Two metal coat hangers

* Wire cutters or tin snips

* Emery paper

Instructions (both the same):

1. Cut the coat hanger once at one end of the longest (bottom) edge, before it bends up towards the shoulder.

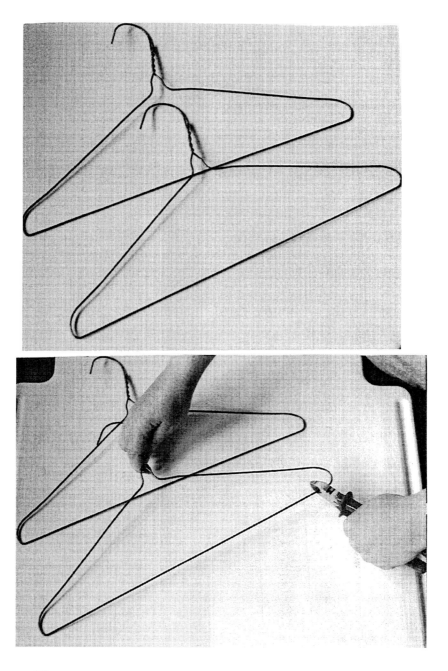

2. Cut the rising edge of the other end half way along the shoulder to make a handle.

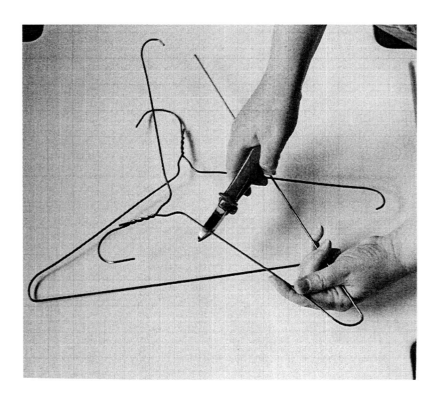

3. Smooth the cut ends with emery paper or similar

4. Bend the handle out at right angles. You now have your dowsing rods.

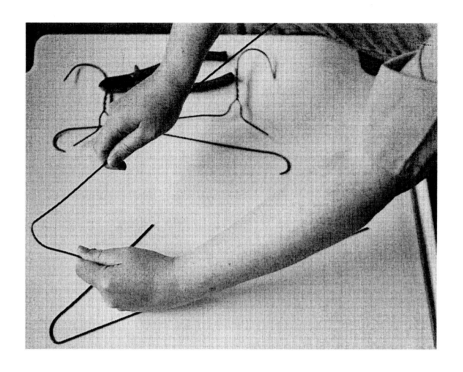

If you want to, you can make them even more simply with welding rods as I did as a child. Just make a right-angle bend three quarters of the way along each rod for your handle and hey presto - you have your dowsing rods!

Dowsing With Rods

* Fill a dish with water.

* Hold your rods loosely, but securely by the handles so that they point forward rather like a gunfighter holding his pistols and can swivel freely.

* Walk towards your dish of water and watch the way the rods move - they often cross.

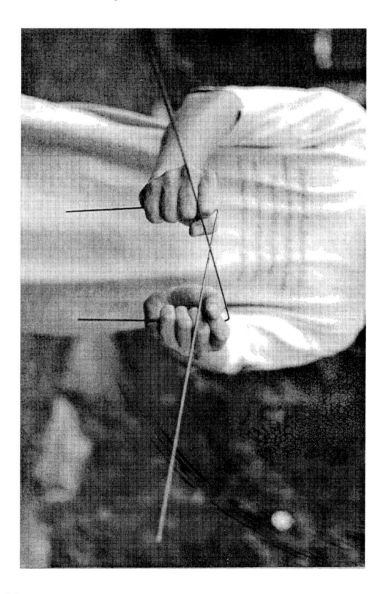

* Now move away from the water and notice the change. Write this down.

* Move around the room, noting the reaction of the rods when you move to the left and right of the water.

When you have tried this a few times and are clear about the signals you are picking up through your dowsing rods, it is time to try a little real dowsing.

* Get some obliging soul to fill a container with water and stand it among a few similar empty ones and cover them all up while you look away, or make a pot of tea. You should not be able to tell which is which.

* Hold the dowsing rods over each container in turn and try to determine which one has water in. The easy way to do this is to say out loud: 'Is there any water in this one?' If you feel silly, just think the question. It should still work.

* Now look away again and ask them to put the dishes in a different order.

* Dowse again as before. You might like to try starting from some distance away and letting the rods lead you to the full container.

Keep this up as long as your assistant's patience lasts. It helps if they want to learn to dowse as well, you can take it in turns.

You may be surprised how many times you are right. If you find the dowsing rods swings on an empty dish, move the dish to another spot and dowse it again. It may be that you have unwittingly divined an underground watercourse. Clever you!

Try with various other things, foods, personal possessions. Avoid stones at this early stage, the dowsing rods tend to react slightly differently to crystalline forms. To begin with you might like to hold a sample of the hidden material in your free hand so that your brain has something to go on. Make sure it is the same and not just of a similar kind or you might end up with a little confusion.

Don't worry if you get it wrong to start with, you are probably trying too hard. Dowsing is a skill of unconscious actions.

Can you ride a bicycle? Cast your mind back to when you first started to learn. You concentrated really hard and the bike wobbled alarmingly. Then, you got used to steering and pedalling and suddenly you weren't thinking of keeping your balance any more. It was coming automatically and the bike ceased to wobble. Dowsing works in the same way. It is perfectly possible to dowse after a fashion whilst concentrating really hard on making the rods react properly, but real success comes when you are no longer worrying about the movements of your dowsing medium and have your attention fixed on the object being dowsed.

If all is going well, you will now be ready to try asking questions that do not have a clear-cut answer. For example, when dowsing your containers, have your 'assistant' fill one and then empty it. Then when you hold your dowsing rods over that container and ask 'does this contain water?' you may find that the dowsing rods move in a different way. You will then have to ask further questions: 'Has this recently contained water;' or 'is this wet?' I'm sure you can think up other variables on the same theme.

Energies can be dowsed with bent wire dowsing rods and the best place to try this is on a known energy line or around standing stones or stone circles.

If you have never investigated stone circles, you are in for some surprises. Energies radiate from the stones in all kinds of directions and different energies course around the circles. Don't just dowse next to the stones, try finding other energy bands inside and outside the circles.

Many serious students of megalithic sites find these rods invaluable and you could find yourself in good company as you stride purposefully across the site.

Dowsers have detected bands of energy running through each stone, which, if they were visible would look like horizontal stripes. They are in pairs of positive and negative, often seven pairs in each stone. These energy bands are not consistent, but change with the seasons. In some cases, these changes occur very frequently. In his book, Needles of Stone, Tom Graves measured the polarities of the Rollright Stone circle in Oxfordshire morning and night for a week. He found significant differences in the stones and in the rate of polarity changes.

Twelve of the stones held the same charge for the whole week, but others had individual cycles, which changed from hour to hour. A few actually changed as often as every twenty seconds.

These energies then link together in complex networks, like the threads of a spider's web, which shift and change according to the interrelation of the individual parts, making an altogether more powerful whole. People spend their entire lives studying these webs of energy and there is still more to discover! The Rollright Stones are

mentioned several times in this book. They are not the only standing stones I have investigated, but I think it is interesting to consider the findings of a number of dowsers working on the same site.

Chapter 4
The Pendulum

A dowsing pendulum can be made in many, many ways. The needle on its thread or the wedding ring on a hair are traditional improvisations. Other makeshift pendulums can be anything from a button on a piece of thread, to a shoulder bag suspended by its handle, though the latter can be difficult to use discreetly and is not particularly responsive for beginners. However if you are out shopping and want to know if a particular food suits you, it is a handy stand in, as is a key on a chain.

What Should the Pendulum Be Made From?

A pendulum for dowsing can be made of almost anything. Many people think that it is necessary to use specific materials for specific purposes. That may be true of active dowsing, I have not found any evidence for it in passive dowsing - which is the kind we are going to begin with. Active dowsing should not be done by beginners, so please don't - at least, not until you understand the process.

The two components of a pendulum are a thread, hinged rod or chain capable of swinging freely and a weight attached to the bottom. Whether that weight be a button on a length of thread, or a crystal on a silver chain is quite irrelevant. It is merely tool, an extension of yourself, so use whatever you are comfortable with, making sure your cord or chain is flexible enough to allow free movement in all directions.

For the last year or so I have been doing a lot of telephone dowsing (explained in chapter 10). Because my pendulum is not always to hand, and the shoe rack is; I've used a black leather boot, a trainer, a walking shoe and almost anything else I could reach that had a lace in it. Boots, though, can have their disadvantages, the swing can be a little erratic in inexperienced hands, and it can tend to kick you in the face if you get a strong reading. Ouch!

So, What Is the Best Kind of Pendulum?

The better balanced your first pendulum is, the easier you will be able to understand the different swings. Use something reasonably symmetrical, an electric pull cord handle, or small plum bob are both ideal. If you want something more personal, you can get spiral findings from some handicraft suppliers into which you can pop a pebble or polished stone and fix this to either a chain, thong or cord.

Keep an open mind when looking for something to practice with. Once I was on holiday and kept wanting to dowse but had nothing suitable with me - all shoes were attached to feet. In one of the gift shops I found a child's necklace for sale. It was in the form of a little wooden doll with a cord fixed to the top of her hat. She was shaped like a little fat skittle, just perfect for dowsing.

Conventional pendulums

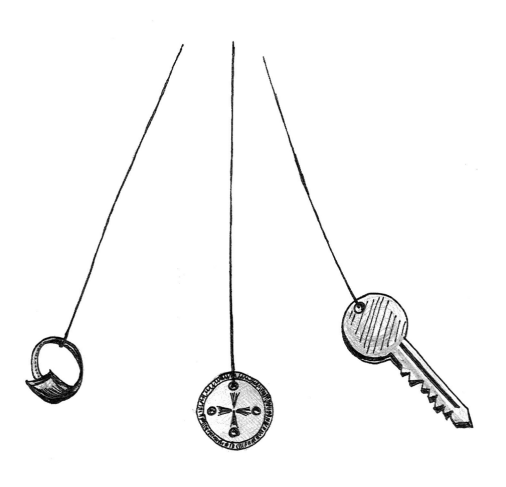

Unconventional pendulums

Her hair was yellow and I called her Tilly Sunshine (we all have our little eccentricities). She was my pendulum for the next two years, until she tragically dropped out of the bottom of her hat. I now often dowse with the hat to which the hair is still attached.

Bald headed Tilly is in retirement and watches the world go by from my kitchen window. Before Tilly I used a pendulum made of yew wood on a length of string and many people asked where it came from, as they wanted to learn to dowse.

The truth was my, yew pendulum might just as well have been made of plastic, or diamonds. The effect would have been exactly the same. I have even dowsed using a suitcase when someone has telephoned with an urgent question just as I was going on holiday. My arm became the cord in this instance. Thankfully they only had one simple question, otherwise I might have suffered muscle strain!

One comment I would make about your first pendulum: the better balanced it is, the easier you will be able to understand the different swings. Large flat pendants tend to be a bit tricky for the novice, as do suitcases, so use something reasonably symmetrical that has a suitable cord or chain.

When you get a bit more practised, symmetry will not be so important, but it always makes life easier, especially when dowsing subjects that only have a very slight effect on the swing.

To Make a Simple Pendulum

Materials:

* A small symmetrical weight around 25-50g - a well shaped pebble is ideal.

* A bell cap from jewellery findings suppliers.

* A cord or chain strong enough to support the weight and flexible enough to swing freely. The length should be a little over 1m for a precise dowsing pendulum. A length of 50 cm is adequate for general purposes. For a pocket pendulum like the one illustrated, a broken necklace can supply the chain and make the job of fixing it altogether easier.

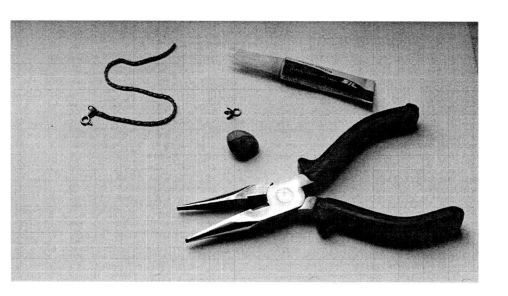

* Needle nosed pliers.

* Strong glue. Super glue was used for this pendulum.

Instructions:

1. Open out the bell cap to fit snugly onto the pebble.

2. Grip the ring of the bell cap with the pliers and apply glue to the area of pebble to which it will be fixed. Be careful not to apply too much - you don't want to glue your fingers to the pebble too (it helps to have a light smear of petroleum jelly on your fingers to guard against getting stuck up).

3. Holding a glue free area of the pebble in one hand press the bell cap into place, taking care that no glue oozes onto the pliers, otherwise you may end up with a very heavy and unwieldy pendulum. Hold until fixed. If the pebble is very well shaped, you might be able to simply press the bell cap onto the top of it and leave it to set.

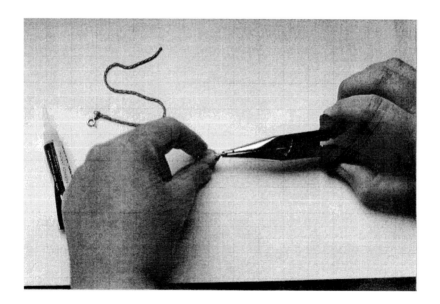

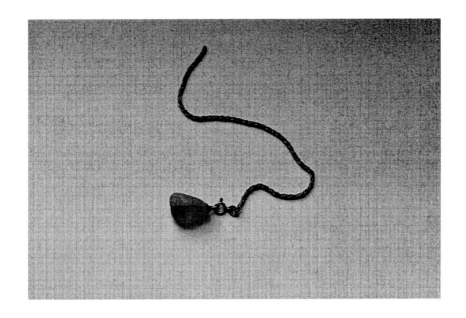

4. Attach your chosen cord or chain. You now have a pendulum.

Dowsing With Your Pendulum

Using a pendulum is my favourite method of passive dowsing. Its swing can give me a lot of information and it is something I can carry in a pocket most of the time, so it is readily available. It is also very easy to improvise.

You are going to learn the art of passive dowsing so take your pendulum, made of whatever you like, and hold it loosely in whichever hand suits you. Have a notebook handy and write down everything you learn. Notes you make now will help with future studies.

To begin with, you might need to set your pendulum swinging deliberately. Once it is moving, start asking some questions. At this stage only ask questions to which the answer is a definite yes or a definite no. Either-or questions will cause confusion and frustration; you won't get a sensible answer. It is best to start with five or six questions to which the answer is yes.

As you ask the questions, either out loud or in your head, watch how the pendulum swings.

Some 'Yes' Questions To Try

* Is my name (your name)?

* Am I male/female (whichever you can answer 'yes' to)?
* Am I a human (assuming you are not from mars)?

* Are my eyes (your eye colour)?

* Do I breathe air?

* Do goldfish live in water?

You get the general idea. Make up your own questions if you like, just don't try to be too clever at this point. Keep the pendulum swinging as you ask the questions and watch to see if the direction of the swing changes. Whether it does or not, make a note. Perhaps you had started it off with what will become your 'yes' swing.

Some 'No' Questions To Try

* Is my name (another name)?

* Am I male/female (whichever you can answer 'no' to)?

* Am I a hamster (assuming you are not a very clever rodent)?

* Are my eyes (another eye colour)?

* Do I breathe water?

* Do goldfish grow leaves?

To begin with, you may not get much reaction. If you get no reaction at all, you are probably trying too hard, or taking yourself too seriously. Persevere, and lighten up. It will come and when it does, remember to make notes. Usually people who have difficulty pendulum dowsing are trying to keep their hand as rigid as possible, sometimes even holding it with their other hand or bracing it against a table or chair back. Others have the same problem I explained with metal rod dowsing and are concentrating on the action of the pendulum, rather than the question they are trying to get answers for. This is to misunderstand the process.

All kinds of dowsing work on signals passed from the cerebellum (rear portion of the brain) through minute muscle movements to the hand. It is thought that the seat of intuition is somewhere in the cerebellum, but it is not linked directly to speech centres or conscious thought in most people, so dowsing is a method of connecting with the intuition. Sometimes you can actually see a dowser's hand moving as the pendulum's swing alters. There is no trickery here, they are simply responding to signals from the cerebellum, which might be very strong.

You might find that just as your intuition starts to come through, you will have a strange tickling sensation in the back of your head. This is by no means universal, but happens quite often, particularly with children. Young boys are especially susceptible to this sensation. Sometimes people feel as if a light has been switched on inside them and others get a tingly feeling in their arms. This is just the link with your intuitive centre switching itself on and is perfectly normal.

It is equally normal to feel nothing at all and still get good results from dowsing, so don't worry either way. The important thing is to find what works for you and make a note of it.

As we have already determined, when the pendulum starts to move, it should swing one way for yes and another for no. This will be individual to you. For me, swinging in a circle means yes, and back and forth means no. For a friend, clockwise is yes, anti-clockwise is no. We are all different. You really do have to take careful note of how it swings for you and you alone.

Practice with questions to which you know the answers until you are clear about how your pendulum swings and what it means.
When you are happy, we can make things a little more interesting. You know how a pendulum swings for a simple 'yes', but sometimes we have questions to which we don't already know the answers and there might be a dozen possibilities. That's when we use dowsing charts. We are going to start with colours.

Copy Chart 1 (overleaf) onto a piece of clean white paper or card.

* Hold your pendulum over the centre (C).

* Set it swinging along the base line (B), keeping it centred over (C).

* Now ask questions that relate to colours. Try eye colour to begin with, then maybe the colour of something you are wearing - so long as it is only a single colour at this stage.

* As the pendulum swings, it should start to alter its swing to travel over the segment marked in the relevant colour.

* When you are confident, we can make it even more interesting by choosing something with more than one colour.

* Set the pendulum swinging and ask what colour the item is. It will swing over one colour and note this down.

* Ask if there is another colour on the item and the swing should alter to show another colour.

* Continue until all colours have been shown.

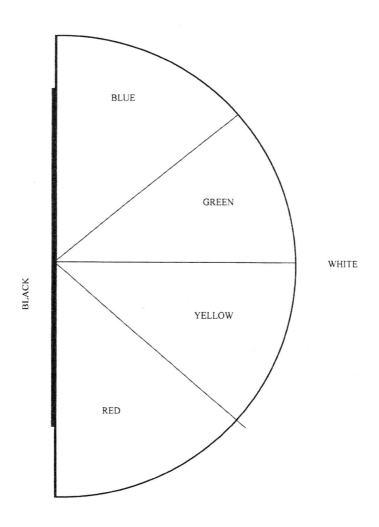

Colours Dowsing Chart

Chapter 5

Polarities and Gender

Positives and negatives of many kinds can be detected with a pendulum. The first kind you already know, but there are also those of polarity and gender. This can be dowsed and works on the polarity of the electromagnetic energy in the body. Men and women are 'poles apart', the static electricity moves in opposite directions. If we were batteries, women would be one way up, men the other.

Hold your pendulum over the head of a friendly female (of any specie, though humans don't try to capture the pendulum like a cat might). Allow your pendulum to swing without any specific question in mind. You will probably notice that the pendulum swing changes, even though you have not asked a question. Repeat the exercise with a friendly male (remember to ask first in both instances). This time, the unasked answer will be different! Try it as many times as you like.

In Britain, a traditional method of determining the sex of their unborn child was to suspend a needle or a wedding ring on a length of sewing thread over the 'bump' and see how it moves. If it rotated, the baby would be a girl, if it swung back and forth, it would be a boy.

At the turn of the century a hand held device was devised for sexing chicks whilst still in the egg using the same principle. It was basically a pendulum in a case that was placed over the egg being tested, and when tested on an antiques show on British television a few years ago, it still worked perfectly.

Pendulums can tell us a lot about the energies in crystalline objects including standing stones and pebbles. Obviously for most people, the pebbles are the most accessible, so here's a little experiment to try.

* Go into your garden or park and collect a few pebbles. It doesn't matter what kind, but the more varied they are, the better.

* Dowse it as you did the dishes of water. For this I am suggesting a pendulum, but don't be afraid to try it with your dowsing rods or forked stick (outside).

When you hold your pendulum over a pebble, you will find that it is either masculine or feminine - remember the man and woman you dowsed? In other words its polarity is either positive or negative. This might be its original polarity, or it may have been changed by the actions of humans at some time past. If a stone is thrown hard at a wall by a man, or held in the hand and hit a few times sharply with a hammer, it will absorb male energy. If the same thing is done by a woman, it will take on female energy.

Naturally as with all rules, there are exceptions. Hematite is a form of pewter grey iron ore with a tint of red that is often cut and polished as a semi-precious stone and used in jewellery. Whenever I hold my pendulum over a piece of this, it ceases to swing at all. I believe this is because it has a magnetic shielding effect.

It certainly works for me to block discordant energies that might otherwise cause me problems.

* Sort the pebbles into masculine and feminine.

* Try dowsing around the perimeter of each stone. You will find that there is a very specific direction to the energy flow of every stone.

* Mark the results down in your trusty notebook.

Curious Cones

Hold the pendulum at different heights above one stone and watch the swing. This is where things begin to get really fascinating. Every stone has a unique conical energy field that surrounds it in a very specific way. The height and radius of the cone will vary according to the size and type of stone and will be mirrored above and below. If you hold your pendulum above the apex of the upper cone, you will discover that another inverted cone is also present. This holds true for stones of all shapes and sizes, including standing stones and even precious gems. You can also place the stone on a raised platform and dowse below it to find yet another conical field. Try it!

Social Stones

Stones react to each other and the situation in which they find themselves.

* Take a number of masculine and feminine stones and arrange them on a tray or table.

* Dowse over and around each stone. Watch how the polarities seem to have changed slightly. There are new

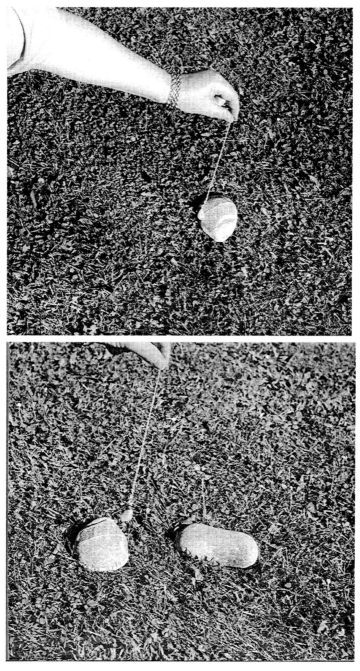

50

energy lines running between the stones, some beneficial, others less so.

* Hold your free hand over each stone in turn and try to determine whether it is 'happy' by dowsing, with your pendulum held away from the arrangement. In this case, the pendulum will be swinging in response to your question rather than to the polarity of the stone.

* Rearrange them, touching each in turn and asking it whether it wants to be there, moving them all until you have a harmonious arrangement.

* Hold your pendulum directly over and around the arrangement of stones and see if you can detect the changes in the individual energy fields of the stones and the new energy lines created by your arrangement.

* Naturally, you should be making copious notes - or at least rough sketches of your findings all the time.

* Move one pebble to a different place and take note of the reaction of it and its fellows. If you are particularly perceptive, you may actually be able to sense the disruption in the energies.

* When you have finished, always return the stones to their preferred positions, or break up the arrangement and put the stones back where they came from.

Chapter 6

Improving Your Environment by Dowsing

Have you ever noticed that every room seems to have its own special character? Some are friendly, some distinctly chilly regardless of the temperature, some calm, and some chaotic. The energies that are all around us also affect the atmosphere of your living space. If you can't settle in your own home, or if you find that apathy seems to rule, then perhaps these energies are unbalanced.

There are things you can do to improve matters.

Create a simple dowsing chart, dividing the semicircle into segments relating to the various possible causes of disharmony. If preferred you can copy the example onto a piece of paper or card.

* Make an accurate, but simple sketch of the room,
  marking windows, mirrors, furniture and plants. It
  doesn't matter if you can't draw, simple shapes to
  denote the objects will suffice.

* Place your dowsing chart in the space you wish to heal and hold your pendulum directly above the central point at the base of the chart and set it swinging, along the straight edge, asking the question:

* What is the main problem with this area?

* If there is a problem the pendulum will swing across the relevant answer. Note this down on your layout sketch.

* Now ask if there is another problem with this area?

* If there is, use your dowsing chart again to ascertain what it is and make a note.

* Continue until you feel you have listed all the problems in that area.

* Move your chart to another part of the room and repeat the exercise. It is as well to dowse several different areas.

Energy disruption can be quite localised and may even be a result of a ley line running right through the building. These lines are sometimes called dragon lines, especially in China. They criss-cross the earth and most cause no problems whatever. There are times, though, particularly where they pass over an underground water table, where the energies become disruptive and need to be checked.

Sometimes the energy disruption is very localised indeed and you may well find that it emanates directly from the arrangement of your possessions. Simply moving the furniture, or tidying up could make a big difference.

Some things tend to deflect the energies in a room or cause all kinds of muddling effects. These include mirrors, beds and fish tanks, and so take care to dowse whether they are in the best possible place. Sometimes you will even find you need to move them to another room altogether.

Once you have determined the problem areas, you can begin to correct the problem.

Firstly, try moving things around, dowsing to find the most suitable site for each. Perhaps you will only need to adjust the angle of some pieces, others might have to be moved completely. You will probably find the new arrangement very easy to live with as harmonised energies begin to flow through the room.

Very occasionally an item will have very disruptive energies and will not improve wherever you put it. If this is the case, try cleansing it either by burning a small twig of rosemary herb in the room so that the smoke curls around the object (please pay close attention to fire safety). If you don't have any fresh rosemary, use an oil evaporator with rosemary in. If smoke or vapours would cause damage, you could try washing the item in running water whilst visualising all disruptive energies flowing out of it into the water and from there into the earth. The method you choose will depend on the troublesome item, so I shall leave that up to you. If none of the above remedies work and you can think of nothing that will, consider disposing of it.

Sometimes the problem stems from outside and slightly different action needs to be taken to deflect harmful energies from the room. A good method is with the use of pebbles.

ROOM PLAN

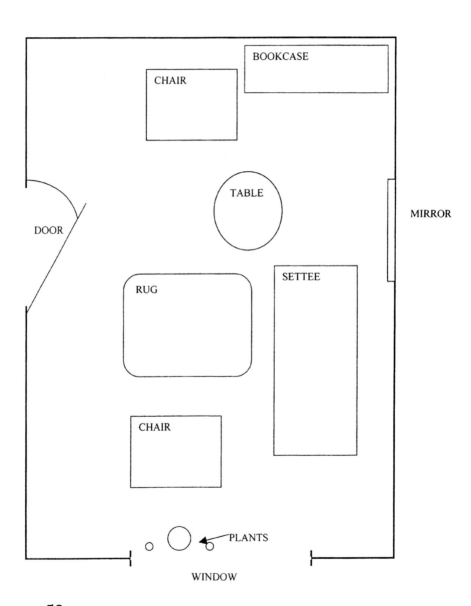

Dowsing Chart For Room Energies

Overly tense atmospheres tend to have an abundance of masculine vibrations. The cure is to place a stone in the room that has a feminine charge. If an area is too relaxed, a masculine charged stone will restore the balance.

If you have detected a disruptive energy line, dowse to find the height of the line. Most energy lines have several layers, alternating between positive and negative, so the height of the centre of the line is important.

When you have determined this, select some small pebbles made from quartz. These may be in the form of sandstone, quartz crystal, or a mixture.

Dowse the stones you have to decide which will work best and place these where the line enters your space.

Place a few more where the line leaves as well. You may need to use a small table or shelf at the right height, or you could put them in a small bag and hang them on the wall. If you decide on the latter, make sure the bag is not made of paper or acrylic fibres, as both are made from wood (this applies to so-called wood free paper too). Wood seems to disable crystals at close range.

Chapter 7

Looking For Lost Property and Buried Treasure

You can use any of the methods outlined in this book to find lost property. You simply have to keep a firm idea in mind of the item you are looking for and either dowse over the area it was thought to have been lost, or draw a plan and dowse over this. When my youngest daughter was two, I had to go to an important meeting and couldn't find my car keys anywhere. The problem was made worse because I was supposed to be giving a lift to some other people who had no other means of transport.

After a fruitless search of the house I resorted to dowsing. The method described below worked extremely well and can be adapted to find almost anything. It turned out that my little one had pushed the keys behind a chair cushion that was stitched in place top and bottom. I hadn't even realised that it was possible to get a hand behind it until I dowsed that my keys were there! Happily we all arrived on time and the meeting went well.

Finding Lost Keys

* Go into each room in turn and ask: 'Are my keys here?' Watch the swing of the pendulum, or movement of the dowsing rods or twig.

* If it is negative, or no reaction occurs move on to the next room.

* If the dowse is positive, walk to each corner in turn and ask: 'Are my keys in this part of the room?'

* Continue to narrow the search down until you find your keys.

* Alternatively, draw a simple plan of the room, marking the positions of furniture and anything else that might conceal what you are looking for. This method is best suited to a pendulum on a short cord.

* Hold your pendulum over the plan, moving from one part to another and asking if your keys are here. If the swing changes, take note and go and look there.

This technique is often very successful and has been extended by industry to use maps to dowse sites of possible oil or coal deposits. Generally, the dowser uses a pendulum over the map, dowsing section by section and marking any positive readings. Occasionally the dowser will hold the pendulum in one hand and move a finger over the map with the other. However it is done, the results have proven so worthwhile that several petrol companies employ professional dowsers and claim to find them more accurate than geological studies!

Chapter 8

Dowsing For Different Substances

It has been discovered that the pendulum reacts differently to different substances. Silver, for instance, will cause a different reaction from iron. Thanks to pioneering work by other dowsers in the last century, especially T. C. Lethbridge and J Havelock Fidler, we now have ways of differentiating between them.

It all has to do with the length of the pendulum cord and the direction of its swing. To try this, you need a reasonably heavy pendulum on a string at least one metre in length. The weight will help prevent your results being affected by strong winds.

* Wind up the pendulum cord to around 45 cm and get the pendulum swinging.

* Gradually lengthen the cord, observing the swing. When it reaches 55 cm, you might just find that the swing changes.

* Try with as many materials as you can and note down the length of the cord that each material reacts to.

This is what T C Lethbridge did. He started off in his study, trying on all kinds of substances, mineral and organic and found that each seemed to cause the pendulum to react in a particular and consistent way. He then went outside, armed with this knowledge, and began to dowse his garden and courtyard with the pendulum set at twenty-two inches, the length for silver. At one spot, the swing changed and he carefully dug down an inch or two to find a piece of seventeenth century pottery. He continued to dig and found a shard of stoneware from the same period. Puzzled, he dowsed the two fragments and found they reacted as if they were silver. It transpired that the glaze contained lead, which has exactly the same dowsing 'rate' as silver! So there, the expert learned something new. He also found that there was an energy field around each object with a radius equal to the rate - so that a piece of silver (or lead) would have a circular energy field with a radius of 55 cm.

Colours, too, can be detected with a pendulum. Yellow and white, for example, have a rate (cord length) of 72.5 cm; blue is 60 cm. Look at the table on the next page and try to add to it by dowsing other substances and colours. Items that fall into two categories have a dual rate - the pendulum will react at either cord length.

Fidler continued this work and finding that he had difficulty with a cord length of a metre in high winds, discovered that exactly opposite results could be obtained if the cord was precisely half, or even a quarter of the lengths specified by Lethbridge. Thus by reversing his expectations, he could draw correct conclusions. Fidler also ascertained that if his cord was too long for the substance being dowsed it would swing from side to side and if too short, it would travel back and forth. This was, of course individual to him, but the basic principals should work for anyone.

Corò Lengths of a Few Substances

(experiment to add to this list)

50 cm   LIFE
               SACRED SITE
               MAGNETIC ROCK

55 cm   SILVER
               LEAD

60 cm   MALES
               DIAMONDS
               THE COLOUR BLUE

72.5 cm   FEMALES
               GOLD
               THE COLOUR YELLOW
               WHITE

100 cm   DEATH
               BLACK

Chapter 9

Dowsing the Great Outdoors

Now that you are such an expert dowser it is time to take your pendulum outside. If you have been using something fairly lightweight, you will need to exchange this for a pendulum that is heavy enough to withstand the odd gust of wind.

The energies you found in your small stones are similar to those flowing through standing stones and stone circles. If you do get the chance to dowse some standing stones, take it. If you live in Britain, no doubt you live within striking distance of one of the many alignments that occur within these isles and a lot of fascinating information can be acquired from these sites by dowsing. Take your pendulum along and give it a try.

A note of caution, though; certain circles, such as the Rollright Stones in Oxfordshire, whilst seemingly small and unprepossessing, have a lot of power running through them. Dowsers have been studying them for decades and those who decided to work in pairs have inadvertently made connections that have resulted in a

strong charge of energy. One researcher took an assistant along to the stones. They stood at different points, one inside, and the other outside the circle, to try and define points of entry and exit of specific lines. As soon as they began, they suffered severe headaches and were unable to continue. Perhaps the fact that there were two of them standing on a line and linked by a common goal made them more sensitive to the powerful energies involved.

This phenomenon does not seem to affect lone dowsers. I recently dowsed the Rollright Stones myself and found all sorts of interesting lines running between the strangely shaped stones, but remained free from headaches. In the middle of the circle, my pendulum was completely still - dead centre as a friend quipped at the time. Did you find the same at the centre of your pebble circle?

If you have no interest in standing stones and their energies, perhaps you might like to use your new skill to find water courses, archaeological sites, lost property in your garden - anything you like, though do obtain permission before going onto someone else's land, even your neighbour's.

Churches have an amazing amount of energy running through them, especially old ones, so if you can get permission, try dowsing your local church. Make a little plan first and note down what you find as you go. Pay particular attention to the altars and the doors. If you thought they were just places people went to on Sunday to sing a song or two, you may be in for a surprise. Bear in mind that many ancient churches stand on ancient sacred sites that were originally chosen for their energies.

Most churches are built from stone and contain stone altars. They often contain many artefacts that have been venerated for a long time and fascinating insights into polarities can be obtained by dowsing in a church. Altars in the main church, for instance, tend to be masculine, where as those in the Lady chapels are almost without exception feminine. Before dowsing in any place of worship, always obtain the permission of the relevant authorities. Great offence can be caused by thoughtless behaviour, however innocuous you might consider it to be.

Chapter 10
Dowsing Health Problems

Allergies account for an awful lot of the problems with the health of the physical body. Dowsing is a good way of identifying allergens and food intolerances. You will then need to go through the foods within the problem groups to identify those that are adversely affecting the person. These should be left out of the diet for at least a month, to completely clear the system, then added back in one at a time, watching for reactions. Some people will have a life long intolerance to certain foods, whilst others will merely need to give their system a rest for a few weeks. In most cases, foods which have caused problems should not be eaten more than once in ten days so that the body does not have chance to rebuild the sensitivity.

Where the number of foods is large, or in the case of a young child, medical advice should be sought before drastically reducing the variety of foods in the diet.

Sometimes it is not what is included in the diet that is the problem, but what is omitted. This can be particularly true with children and the elderly, whose appetite may not be large and whose tastes might be limited. Dietary supplements can be truly life enhancing when taken by people who need them. These can include vitamins, minerals and fish oils. Another worthwhile supplement to dowse for is garlic. Its benefits have been well known for centuries and in Siberia, it was so highly valued that its price in barter was equal to a sable fur - the most expensive fur available there.

Sometimes a food that suits us for breakfast will not be at all good for us in the middle of the day, so it is good to include a time factor in when dowsing foods and food supplements. It isn't enough to determine whether a person needs toast and jam, for example, they also need to know when they should eat it, and what drink would be best suited to it. I have been surprised at the results of this kind of dowse. One lady could eat tomatoes, she could eat mushrooms, but she could only eat them together at seven in the evening. Another could eat tuna and mayonnaise at midday, but would bloat if she ate it half an hour later. We really do change from one minute to the next, so if food sensitivity is a real problem, examine all aspects of the situation. This lady was very prone to bloating if she ate the wrong things at the wrong times. She had always avoided chocolate, but through dowsing found that eaten at the right times, this would actually relieve the bloating completely!

You will find that you can make life a lot easier by dietary dowsing, but prepare for some surprises. I used to regularly dowse a young man who was suffering from Candida Albicans, a stubborn yeast infection of the intestines. At the time, a standard Candida diet precluded any sugar, yeast, or sweet fruit. He was feeling under the weather and through dowsing we ascertained that he needed Marmite (yeast extract) and fresh strawberries, though not at the same times. We got permission from his specialist to let him try these things (which should have made his candida worse), on condition that they were discontinued the moment any adverse reaction presented itself. Instead the young man improved noticeably and enjoyed a treat at the same time!

When dowsing health and dietary matters, it is important to remember your limitations. You may be able to pick up a great deal of information through your pendulum, but only qualified physicians are competent to diagnose specific medical conditions. Don't get above yourself. There is another reason not to try to diagnose specific conditions: though dowsing is good, it is not one hundred percent accurate. People who fear they have a terminal illness are sometimes afraid to consult their doctor. How much easier to have someone hold their hand and swing a pendulum. Do you want that kind of responsibility? An error could ruin somebody's life, and since you are not qualified to comprehend the nature of the illness, how do you expect to dowse it accurately? Diagnostic dowsing does have its place, but that place is with the professionals, not with laypeople.

To dowse food sensitivities, ask the subject to make a list of everything they have eaten and drunk over the course of a month, or at least a week. This should include tap water, sweets, crisps, and daily beverages.

* Read through the list item by item, asking them to imagine the food or drink in their mouth.

* Mark down any your pendulum reacts to, and note whether the reaction is mild or strong - this can have a bearing on just how sensitive the person is to this substance.

* Go back to each of the items reacted to and ask whether this is an allergy.

* If not, ask if it is a sensitivity.

* Check whether they can eat it at any particular times of day, or whether they would be better off switching brands, or variety.

* Dowse whether they have eaten or drunk too much of the particular item and then if they should omit it from their diet for a day, week, or month.

* Continue until all items have been checked and categorised.

Telephone Dowsing

I've mentioned distance and telephone dowsing earlier in the book, so it's only fair that I should explain what I mean.

From time to time, people have needed to consult me, but have been unable to get to my treatment room due to basic logistical problems. One person travelled two hundred miles for a consultation, others come from overseas. Obviously it isn't practical to cover those distances just to check whether a sensitivity has built up to milk or wheat. I discovered quite early on in my career that I could dowse by sound.

I'll give you an example. The lady who has problems with bloating if she eats something at the wrong time needed to contact me several times through the day to ensure that she was safe to eat or drink what she intended. This was particularly important to her if she was planning to go out and wanted to wear smart, fitted clothes. As she lived in London and I have my treatment rooms in the midlands, this presented a problem.

The solution was for her to telephone me and ask the basic dowsing questions whilst I dowsed and passed on the answers. The slight changes in the sound of her voice when she said things that didn't suit her gave my intuition the required information. At any rate, it has proven very accurate.

Here are a few that worked well for her.

* Will a cheese sandwich with butter and pickle be good for me?

* Should I eat it now?

* Should I eat it in ten minutes?

* When I go out tonight, can I drink cider?

* Would lemonade be better?

If she was bloated from eating the wrong thing (I can't be there to answer calls twenty-four hours a day), she would ask something like:

* Will a cup of coffee with two biscuits help unbloat me?

* Can I drink gin and tonic tonight?

As you can see, we have a fairly good idea of what works for her, and the so-called unhealthy things actually do her good at certain times, but substances like coffee can relieve the bloating sometimes and increase it at others, so she finds she needs to check.
The lady is currently teaching her boyfriend to dowse so that she can be less dependent on me. She has tried to dowse herself, but finds that her desires and cravings can tend to influence the swing. This is not true for everyone and you may well find that you can dowse your own needs quite efficiently.

Chapter 11

The Energies Involved in Active Dowsing

After all the dire warnings about diagnostic dowsing, you will be pleased to know there is something you can do. Much of our health is governed by the flow of energy through our bodies. A lot of it works on minute electro-magnetic impulses. With any kind of electrical activity, it is possible for short circuits to occur, confusing and weakening the flow. The flow of energy has a subtle effect on our health, and problems here can eventually lead to illness.

Active dowsing is a method of healing the energy flow of the body by deliberately influencing the swing of a pendulum. For active dowsing, the make-up of the pendulum is more important as it has to have an effect of its own and you will deliberately direct the way it swings. In this case, the most popular is indeed clear crystal, but this is not right or necessary for every occasion.

Test your favourite pendulum by holding the subject's hand and asking if it is suitable for active dowsing of this person. If it is, all well and good, you may continue. If not, try a number of different pendulums; yew wood, quartz, amethyst and amber are good starting points. Until you have found a suitable pendulum, do not continue any further.

Chapter 12

The Flow of Energy and the Chakras

There are energy lines running up and down our own bodies and through energy centres known as chakras. One set of lines run between our heads and our feet. They are relatively straight when we are healthy, but can tend to get tangled or diverted when all is not well. Stress or illness can cause problems in the energy lines, which in turn can cause further problems with health. Polarity of men and women is different and opposite and this is reflected in the chakras.

Each chakra has a specific position and purpose in the body. For those not accustomed to visualising pure energy, it is difficult to imagine chakras in any meaningful way. Traditional Ayurvedic teachings were designed for rural, non-technical people and encourage us to think of them as flower buds with whirling petals. To open a chakra, we have to focus our energy on it and imagine the flower bud opening. To close it we reverse the process.

In the west the chakras are often described as vortices of pure energy that rotate at different speeds, the slowest being the root chakra and the fastest, the crown chakra.

The root chakra is a red, four petalled flower. This chakra is at the foundation of the body's energy flow and is situated just above the pubic bone. If it does not work properly, the others cannot. It directly affects the life force and the balance of physical energy and sense of smell. A healthy root chakra will be indicated by a natural vitality and a person who is at ease with the physical world. Problems with the root chakra, such as a blockage of energy will cause listlessness, nerve disorders, and lower backache. The emotions could also be affected with feelings of insecurity, frustration, anger, and depression. The root chakra is the slowest moving of all the chakras.

The spleen chakra is an orange, six petalled flower relating to a balanced sexual appetite, neither excessive nor lacking and the sense of taste. Imbalances in this chakra can be indicated by problems with kidneys, spleen, digestion, and arthritis. There is sometimes an unhealthy attitude to sex, which can either be lacking completely, coupled with an aversion to close physical contact and signs of affection; or excessive, without desire for love or commitment. Other emotional indications of disharmony may be negativity, phobias and lack of energy. This chakra is the second slowest and is situated just below the navel.

The solar plexus chakra is a yellow, ten petalled flower. It relates to the sense of taste and to the psychological aspect of emotions. This is where we experience 'butterflies in the tummy' and the physical aspect is concerned with the circulation and intestinal health. The solar plexus chakra is also linked to healing energies. It

76

moves faster than those below, more slowly than those above.

The heart chakra is a green, twelve petalled flower, and the central chakra, located centrally in the chest. It is concerned with emotions and the sense of touch. When a piece of music moves us to tears, it has touched the heart chakra. This is the centre of unconditional love and allows us to love ourselves, our families, friends, and fellow creatures without expecting anything in return. Disturbances in the flow of energy through this chakra will show up as selfishness, spite, cold heartedness, greed, and envy. Physical problems may include ulcers, palpitations and high or low blood pressure. It moves at medium speed.

The throat chakra is a blue, sixteen petalled flower. It is concerned with communication and the hearing sense, the respiratory tract and joints. This is the centre of self expression and awareness of your own wants and needs and motivation. When energy is flowing smoothly through the throat chakra you are able to take control of your own life and accept the resulting responsibility. Dysfunction can lead to a inability to express or even recognise your own wishes, causing feelings of negativity, blaming others for your own failures and being selfish or over possessive. This chakra is situated at the base of the throat and moves faster than those below it.

The third eye chakra is a violet flower in the centre of the forehead, where the third eye is said to exist. There is disagreement on whether this is a two or many petalled flower. When I meditated on the chakras, I found myself visualising it as a petunia; a trumpet shaped flower with fused petals. It is the chakra of insight and the link between mind and thought. Though the third eye is traditionally thought to be able to see otherworldly things,

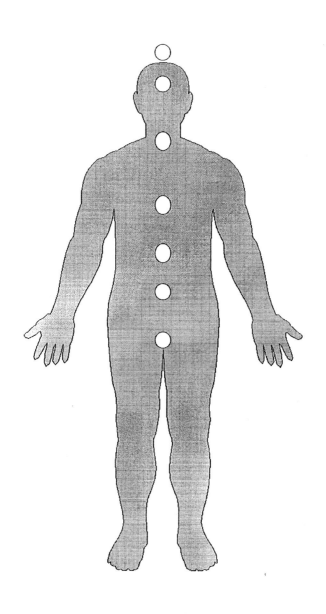

The Chakras

it is also the link to reality and clear thinking. A balanced energy flow through this chakra will allow your creative side to work properly. Imbalances can cause mental confusion, arrogance, and obsessiveness. Physical indicants of problems with this chakra are linked mostly to the head and include ear, nose, and throat disorders insomnia, headaches and eye complaints.

The crown chakra is a white flower just above the top of the head and is linked to spirit and experience. It has more than one thousand petals and is linked to the spirit, harmonising the energies of all the chakras. Through it, the spiritual energies of the cosmos are said to enter our bodies during prayer and healing. When the energy is flowing through this chakra properly, a sense of purpose will pervade your life. You will feel in harmony with the world and capable of true spirituality that has nothing to do with religious dogma. Dysfunction can cause problems with the spiritual side of your nature, perhaps a loss of faith, lack of interest in anything but the strictly material. You may suffer from hyperactivity, migraines, or lowered immunity to disease.

The chakras do not turn all in the same direction, but alternate, like interlocking cogwheels. Their turning is also decided by the gender of the person. As we have already seen, the energy flow in men is the opposite of that in women and the chakras follow this pattern.

In a man, the crown and root chakras turn clockwise, with the others alternating between them. In women, the crown and root chakras turn anti-clockwise.

For a lot of westerners, visualising spinning petals is difficult. It can be easier to imagine the chakras as the cogs in an engine or watch. The teeth interlock and as one turns, it moves the cog above and the one below in the opposite direction. Thus, if the bottom cog turns clockwise, the next turns anti-clockwise and so on. The root chakra moves slowly, so the cog would be fairly large. The wheel above moves slightly quicker, so would need to be smaller, so that its outer rim has to travel a shorter distance to make one revolution and so each spins more quickly than the one below. The crown chakra would be a very tiny, white wheel, spinning so quickly that it is just a blur.

When they are all working and interlocking as they should, the life-engine of mind, body, spirit, and emotion will work perfectly. If one gear is out of sync, it will cause problems with all of the others, affecting the running of the life-engine.

Because you are involving yourself with these energies, it will be necessary to insulate yourself from them to a degree - rather like wearing rubber gloves for cleaning or switching off the power before changing a light bulb. When studying energies and using them to assist the healing process, you will be opening yourself to the unseen powers and energies surrounding you. Healing tends to involve contact with a lot of unbalanced energy and you will very likely find this imbalance affecting your own energies.

Psychic insulation consists of a series of exercises designed to put a barrier between your energy field and that of the person you are helping. If you don't, you might find yourself acting as a kind of radio receiver, taking in the signals emitted by your subject. When this happens, the signal tends to get fixed and you will pick up all manner of problems from them, from nervous tension to other far more serious complaints. I did not fully comprehend this aspect of healing when I first started out and found myself absorbing the problems of others. I'd never had tinnitus before I helped someone suffering from this distressing condition, but I did for a good six months afterwards. A colleague had exactly the same experience, so remember: if someone comes to you seeking help for noises in the ears - insulate yourself!

Chapter 13

Methods of Psychic Insulation

Make yourself comfortable. You may wish to sit, stand, or lie. It isn't important, but if sitting or standing, make sure your feet are flat on the floor. You should make sure you keep 'both feet on the ground' throughout any treatment you may give. Thus you will be well grounded or earthed. Harmful energies will be able to pass through you into the earth, rather than becoming trapped within your own energy field. Equally, your own energies cannot be drained away. This rule applies whatever healing technique you have chosen to use and not just to stone healing. The job of any healer is to channel healing energies to those in need. The energies should come through, not from you. If this point is not heeded, you will soon feel drained and your life force sapped.

There are a number of protective techniques you can employ, some simple, some complex.

Prayer

* Simply say a little prayer to whatever divinity you worship, asking for protection.

White Light

* Imagine yourself bathed in a sphere of white light, which allows you to see out, but shields you from all harm. This is very simple, but it works!

Spiral Protection

* Visualise white light coming up from the ground in a clockwise direction, to spiral around you up over your head, then down again into the ground.

* Imagine this light continually spiralling upwards to your head, then back down into the earth, forming a protective field around you.

The Seven Breaths

This is the most potent protection I know. It not only insulates, but helps you to be in harmony with the elements. It is easiest to do sitting or standing.

* Be aware of your body, of your breathing. Close your eyes if it helps.

* Breathe in slowly. As you inhale, imagine a white light coming up out of the ground behind you, rising to a point above your head.

* Hold the breath for a moment, then breath out, visualising the light descending in front of you, to re-enter the ground as you finish exhaling, leaving behind a glowing arc of white light.

* Pause again before repeating six times more, making seven breaths and seven arcs of white light in all.

* On the next inhalation, imagine the white light coming up to your left and rising in the same way as before, to pause above your head and return to earth to your right.

* Again, pause and repeat a further six times.

* Feel these arcs spinning and rotating to form a sphere of moving light, which will shield you from all harm.

Blue Light

Dark blue light can be used in the same way as white light to provide protection.

* Simply imagine wrapping a dark blue cape around you.

Chapter 14

Healing by Active Dowsing

Once you have mastered the arts of dowsing and of psychic insulation, you can begin to learn to use your pendulum to deliberately adjust polarities within the body.

Because this is an active and deliberate realignment of basic energies, please remember that it can only be done at the behest of the person you are trying to help. No matter how well meaning your actions, you have no right to affect another person unless they want you to - not even a baby. You should also remember that when dowsing anyone, the questions must come from them, or at least be approved by them.

A young man I know learned to dowse, then asked a question about the person he was dowsing without their permission - he caused this person a great deal of distress and did nothing for the reputation of the art.

Please, control your curiosity and retain your integrity.

So, with the permission of the subject, take their hand, arm, foot or whatever is convenient (a little decorum, please!) and dowse to see if you can actually help. You should get a straightforward yes or no.

Ask your subject to lie down comfortably and take up your pendulum.

Once you have created a protective field around yourself, you are ready to make use of the healing energies from above and beneath you, which will flow through you and your pendulum into the energies of your subject.

Always remember that you are a channel, a kind of aerial to direct the energies for the benefit of others, not a battery. These energies should be coming through you, not from you. To do this is to actually give away your own life force and will ultimately damage your health. Another disadvantage of passing on your own energies could be that you also pass on your problems to the subject, which is completely unfair.

It is time now to connect to the energy source of the earth in order to harmonise the energies of the subject. This is often easier said than done for many people and a simple visualisation can be very helpful at this point.

The tree is a traditional symbol of the connection between the various levels of existence. The roots reach deep into the underworld (not to be confused with hell), where they connect directly to the electromagnetic field of the earth, the trunk stands in middle earth where we have our existence, and the branches reach up to the upper or spiritual realm. To visualise yourself as a tree is a good way of connecting to these realms.

* Stand with your feet flat on the ground and visualise roots growing down into the earth. It doesn't matter where you are, even a penthouse has its foundations in the earth. Your roots can grow down from any height.

* Imagine now, branches growing up from the top of your head through your crown chakra. Feel them catching the breeze. Let them connect to the sky. Remember those music and movement classes when you were five? Be that tree.

* Breathe in slowly and steadily.

* As you inhale, let the energy from the earth flow upward through your roots, up through your body and out of the branches at the top of your head.

* Breathe out, letting the energy flowing through the branches drop down again into the earth to complete the circuit.

* Repeat.

* You are a channel, a connector. Let the energy flow through you. It is not of you. You are going to allow the energies to flow through you to the pendulum, through the pendulum to your subject.

* As the cosmic energies flow through your subject, let their own confused energies flow out into the earth in equal measure.

* Keep the energies flowing smoothly. Maintain firm contact with the floor through your feet.

* Place your free hand, over each chakra in turn and dowse to see if it is working properly. Using the following questions. Make notes of the results.

Questions

* Is this chakra working properly

If not:

* Is it moving too slowly?

* Is it moving too quickly?

* Is it moving in the wrong direction for this person's wellbeing?

* If you have found any problems, take the subject's hand again and dowse to see whether you can use active dowsing to help them.

* If so, check that your pendulum is suitable (just ask and dowse the answer).

* If it is, hold it directly over the problem chakra and set it rotating in the correct direction (either clockwise or anti-clockwise according to chakra and gender of subject).

* If the chakra is moving too slowly or quickly, rotate the pendulum whilst concentrating on encouraging the chakra to move at the correct speed.

* If the chakra has gone into reverse, rotate the pendulum in the correct direction. Be sure you get this right; some people are neither entirely male nor entirely

female and this could be reflected in the natural action of their chakras. This is why you must dowse to find what is right for the individual. Personal prejudices have no place in healing.

* Continue until all unbalanced chakras have been treated in the best interests of the subject.

* Now go back and check each chakra again by holding your hand over each in turn and dowsing.

* Continue until you have all chakras in harmony.

* After each session is complete, Draw back the roots and branches you sent out.

* Close your subject's energy centres down, imagining each chakra shutting securely. You might like to visualise this by imagining each chakra as a flower bud closing tightly. If this has no relevance for you, imagine each chakra has a zip and zip it tightly shut.

* Begin with the root chakra and finish by closing the crown chakra.

* Do the same for yourself. Don't skimp here, do the job properly, it takes only a few moments.

* Next, visualise a door or curtains closing between you and the recipient, allowing the healing energies to fall back into the earth.

* To finish, draw the white light closely around you like a cloak and complete the separation between yourself and the person you have been helping.

* Leave no connection. It will not help them and it may harm you.

* Afterwards, go and wash your hands in cold running water to rid your aura of the last traces of any connection, or negative energies.

Ethics are very important when helping people. The Hippocratic oath is very ancient and is sworn by many doctors in the medical profession. One of its tenets is confidentiality. Anything told to a doctor is private and will not be divulged under normal circumstances. You must treat your subject to exactly this guarantee of confidentiality. Healing is personal and private. You may not repeat anything you are told without permission. You may not boast that you have helped such and such a person, even if the results were spectacular and they are the most famous movie star on the face of the planet. Remember that you were a channel for the healing energies of the earth. You simply performed a function. There is nothing to boast about.

Chapter 15

Dowsing, Divining, Divination and Things That Go Bump in the Night

There is sometimes a little confusion between divining and divination since they both come from the same root word. Both relate to discovering information not readily available, but where divining has its place in the solid world of matter, divination belongs to the world of ether - the subtle realm that exists alongside our own where past, present and future have rather less rigid definitions.

Though subtly different in meaning and use, the two are not incompatible.

If you have ever read tarot cards, or the runes, you will know that for each spread of cards or cast of stones there may be a multitude of possible interpretations. Most of those involved in divination have a well developed psychic sense and can see fairly clearly which interpretation is relevant. When learning, though, it can be hard to decide whether it is your intuition that is telling you that the person you are reading for is about to get their come-uppance for something bad they did in the past, or their just reward for something good. This is where dowsing can help. It's also useful for even the most professional reader when intuition is not quite enough.

Many people who present themselves and ask for a reading assume that the reader is so psychic that they already know everything about everyone; past, present and future. So they sit there, silent and expectant, awaiting pronouncements about their life, loves and the best way for them to get rich and famous, whilst being careful not to give any information away, lest this psychic be a charlatan. Now, I admit there are fakes out there, far fewer than you might think, but they do exist. However, in order to find their way through the tangle of information available, even the most psychic person needs to have a little feedback, if only so that they can know they are on the right track.

Where this is not forthcoming, dowsing can help immeasurably. When I give a reading and am not sure that I've got it right, I do a simply dowse on the question 'have I interpreted this correctly?' The cards, runes, or whichever device being used are rather like signposts, they point us in the right direction, but we never know what we might find and occasionally the interpretation is very far from the textbook meaning.

As a matter of interest, I mentioned that there are fewer fakes than might be thought because a few people I have met who openly confess to being fraudulent psychics or healers actually do possess these abilities. The problem is often that they have so little confidence in themselves, or have been brought up to scoff at the notion of all things mystical that they tell themselves that the whole thing is just a scam to make money. Any correct predictions are the result of luck and auto suggestion. The odd thing is, they tend to be right a large proportion of the time.

I once met a very famous British actor who was amused by my activities as a healer and joked that he used to do a bit of faith healing for fun. He found it hilarious that people claimed that his 'mumbo jumbo' made them feel better. Of course this could have just been an example of the placebo effect, but this man is an actor with a great presence - people sense when he walks into a room. His aura spreads out much further than that of most people. This is why he is so good at his job. Actors call it projection - projecting the voice and the emotions out into the audience. I suspect that this projection works on the same wavelength as the healing energies, though I have yet to investigate this properly. In any case, having met him and sensed his energies at close range, I am quite sure that he is a natural healer who is unaware of his gift.

Psychic gifts can come in all shapes and forms. Some people can intuitively know when a friend needs help and knows what kind of help to give; others can heal by touch; almost everyone can dowse, given the right tools and an open mind. There are some who can detect the presence of entities from other realms and also imprints made on places by events that have happened there.

T.C. Lethbridge, the dowser mentioned earlier in this book was out with his wife Mina gathering seaweed at Ladram Beach on a damp and misty day when he encountered a strangely depressing atmosphere, like a blanket of gloom covering the whole beach. He did not mention this to his wife, who had gone further down the beach. Not long afterwards she came hurrying back urging him to leave as she couldn't stand the place, saying that there was 'something frightful' there. The couple returned to the beach on another day and investigated the whole area. At one end two small streams run down and it was here that Mina had had the feeling of some awful presence. Lethbridge felt it too and described it as the feeling you get when suffering from a high fever and full of drugs. The sensation was even worse at the top of the cliff above and his wife said she had an odd feeling as though someone or something was urging her to jump off. Many years later he discovered that a man had committed suicide there nine years before their first visit. He concluded that the atmosphere was the result of the emotions of this unfortunate occurrence that had left a magnetic imprint on the area, rather like that of a magnetic tape or computer disk. The atmosphere was very localised - he could literally walk in and out of it within a few paces. This seemed to work rather like the field of a magnet. If you put a pin on the ground and gradually bring a magnet towards it, nothing will happen until the pin enters the magnetic field, when it will quite literally jump up and attach itself to the magnet. It seems to be the same with the area with this depressing atmosphere - there is no sensation until you are suddenly inside the field. These fields show up very well when dowsed and can form yet another basis for investigation by dowsing.

From time to time, people claim to be able to communicate with beings from other astral planes. If you are open minded enough to accept that this is not the only reality, then I can show you how it is possible to dowse the presence of such entities.

First, insulate yourself with one of the techniques explained in Chapter 12, or use your own preferred method. I generally find that those using white light are the most effective in this situation.

Either use dowsing rods around the room to identify areas of differing energies, or use your pendulum and ask suitable questions. I have listed a few below, but so long as you stick to basic yes/no questions, you can make up your own. Please remember that though you cannot necessarily see these creatures, they can see and understand you, so show a little respect and consideration. I have been in rooms where literally dozens of these beings have been present. They were attracted by a young man whose own chaotic energies had opened the door to the other realm and they had literally popped in for a visit and to see what this world was like. He wanted to know what they were and how to get rid of them - he felt he had had his privacy invaded. We communicated with several of the creatures before politely asking them to leave. I then taught the young man how to control his energies by use of the psychic insulation techniques. He now has a friendly dragon that visits now and again, but is no longer troubled by multiple visitors.

Questions
(remember to insulate yourself before beginning)

* Is there a presence in this room?

* If so: is the presence friendly?

* If so: do you wish to communicate with us?

* Are you here to visit one particular person?

* Continue with your questioning. If the pendulum gyrates in an odd way, you have probably asked a question you had no right to ask. Apologise and change your tack.

* At the end, thank the being or beings and ask them now to return to their own realm or plane of existence.

* Dowse to check that all of them have left, then visualise a door closing and locking securely behind them.

Sometimes the entities are simply spirits of the place, linked to the earth at that particular point. Other times, they can be likened to guardian angels and are present to give advice, warnings, or simple support to a particular individual they consider to be in need. Also, some entities visit just for the sake of it and can become a nuisance if allowed to remain. The important thing is to ask them to return to their own realm at the end of the conversation. Visualise a door closing securely behind them that you control from this side.

Chapter 16

In Conclusion

You now have a fairly good grounding in the various forms of dowsing and divining, both active and passive. Perhaps you will find it useful, perhaps not, though I hope that it will start you off on a whole new life adventure.

The instructions contained in this book represent starting points, nothing more. The adventure is still out there waiting for you and no doubt you will discover many new avenues to explore once you get started.

Whether you simply want to dowse for lost keys or to help someone else is entirely up to you.

There are no rules governing what you can and can't dowse other than those of common sense and decency. You will find, though, that if you consistently try to misuse the technique, your dowsing skills will become very unreliable, and deservedly so.

I ask that you retain your integrity at all times whilst dowsing. You have learned the art from me and I shall be held partly responsible in the cosmic scheme of things if you abuse your knowledge. That said, I'm sure you will use your abilities responsibly and have a lot of fun at the same time.

Happy dowsing!

Bíblíographฆ

Personal Power by Anna Franklin (Capall Bann 1998)

Harper's Encyclopedia of Mystical and Paranormal Experience by Rosemary Ellen Guiley (Harper 1991)

Earth Energy A dowser's Investigation of Ley Lines by J Havelock Fidler (Aquarian Press 1988)

World Famous Strange but True by Colin, Damon and Rowan Wilson (Parragon 1996)

FREE DETAILED CATALOGUE

Capall Bann is owned and run by people actively involved in many of the areas in which we publish. A detailed illustrated catalogue is available on request, SAE or International Postal Coupon appreciated. **Titles can be ordered direct from Capall Bann, post free in the UK** (cheque or PO with order) or from good bookshops and specialist outlets. Titles include:

A Breath Behind Time, Terri Hector
Angels and Goddesses - Celtic Christianity & Paganism, M. Howard
Arthur - The Legend Unveiled, C Johnson & E Lung
Astrology The Inner Eye - A Guide in Everyday Language, E Smith
Auguries and Omens - The Magical Lore of Birds, Yvonne Aburrow
Asyniur - Womens Mysteries in the Northern Tradition, S McGrath
Begonnings - Geomancy, Builder's Rites & Electional Astrology in the
    European Tradition, Nigel Pennick
Between Earth and Sky, Julia Day
Book of the Veil , Peter Paddon
Caer Sidhe - Celtic Astrology and Astronomy, Vol 1, Michael Bayley
Caer Sidhe - Celtic Astrology and Astronomy, Vol 2 M Bayley
Call of the Horned Piper, Nigel Jackson
Cat's Company, Ann Walker
Celtic Faery Shamanism, Catrin James
Celtic Faery Shamanism - The Wisdom of the Otherworld, Catrin James
Celtic Lore & Druidic Ritual, Rhiannon Ryall
Celtic Sacifice - Pre Christian Ritual & Religion, Marion Pearce
Celtic Saints and the Glastonbury Zodiac, Mary Caine
Circle and the Square, Jack Gale
Compleat Vampyre - The Vampyre Shaman, Nigel Jackson
Creating Form From the Mist - The Wisdom of Women in Celtic Myth and
    Culture, Lynne Sinclair-Wood
Crystal Clear - A Guide to Quartz Crystal, Jennifer Dent
Crystal Doorways, Simon & Sue Lilly
Crossing the Borderlines - Guising, Masking & Ritual Animal Disguise in the
    European Tradition, Nigel Pennick
Dragons of the West, Nigel Pennick
Earth Dance - A Year of Pagan Rituals, Jan Brodie
Earth Harmony - Places of Power, Holiness & Healing, Nigel Pennick
Earth Magic, Margaret McArthur
Eildon Tree (The) Romany Language & Lore, Michael Hoadley
Enchanted Forest - The Magical Lore of Trees, Yvonne Aburrow

100

Everything You Always Wanted To Know About Your Body, But So Far
Nobody's Been Able To Tell You, Chris Thomas & D Baker
Face of the Deep - Healing Body & Soul, Penny Allen
Fairies in the Irish Tradition, Molly Gowen
Familiars - Animal Powers of Britain, Anna Franklin
Fool's First Steps, (The) Chris Thomas
Forest Paths - Tree Divination, Brian Harrison, Ill. S. Rouse
Gardening For Wildlife Ron Wilson
God Year, The, Nigel Pennick & Helen Field
Goddess on the Cross, Dr George Young
Handbook For Pagan Healers, Liz Joan
Handbook of Fairies, Ronan Coghlan
Healing Book, The, Chris Thomas and Diane Baker
Healing Homes, Jennifer Dent
Healing Stones, Sue Philips
Herb Craft - Shamanic & Ritual Use of Herbs, Lavender & Franklin
Hidden Heritage - Exploring Ancient Essex, Terry Johnson
In Search of Herne the Hunter, Eric Fitch
Intuitive Journey, Ann Walker Isis - African Queen, Akkadia Ford
Journey Home, The, Chris Thomas
Language of the Psycards, Berenice
Legend of Robin Hood, The, Richard Rutherford-Moore
Lid Off the Cauldron, Patricia Crowther
Light From the Shadows - Modern Traditional Witchcraft, Gwyn
Living Tarot, Ann Walker
Lore of the Sacred Horse, Marion Davies
Lost Lands & Sunken Cities (2nd ed.), Nigel Pennick
Magic of Herbs - A Complete Home Herbal, Rhiannon Ryall
Magical Guardians - Exploring the Spirit and Nature of Trees, Philip Heselton
Magical History of the Horse, Janet Farrar & Virginia Russell
Magical Lore of Animals, Yvonne Aburrow
Magical Lore of Cats, Marion Davies
Magick Without Peers, Ariadne Rainbird & David Rankine
Masks of Misrule - Horned God & His Cult in Europe, Nigel Jackson
Medicine For The Coming Age, Lisa Sand MD
Medium Rare - Reminiscences of a Clairvoyant, Muriel Renard
Mind Massage - 60 Creative Visualisations, Marlene Maundrill
Mirrors of Magic - Evoking the Spirit of the Dewponds, P Heselton
Moon Mysteries, Jan Brodie
Mysteries of the Runes, Michael Howard
Mystic Life of Animals, Ann Walker
New Celtic Oracle The, Nigel Pennick & Nigel Jackson
Pagan Feasts - Seasonal Food for the 8 Festivals, Franklin & Phillips
Patchwork of Magic - Living in a Pagan World, Julia Day
Pathworking - A Practical Book of Guided Meditations, Pete Jennings
Personal Power, Anna Franklin

Practical Divining, Richard Foord
Practical Meditation, Steve Hounsome
Psychic Self Defence - Real Solutions, Jan Brodie
Real Fairies, David Tame
Reality - How It Works & Why It Mostly Doesn't, Rik Dent
Romany Tapestry, Michael Houghton
Runic Astrology, Nigel Pennick
Sacred Animals, Gordon MacLellan
Sacred Celtic Animals, Marion Davies, Ill. Simon Rouse
Sacred Dorset - On the Path of the Dragon, Peter Knight
Sacred Grove - The Mysteries of the Forest, Yvonne Aburrow
Sacred Geometry, Nigel Pennick
Sacred Nature, Ancient Wisdom & Modern Meanings, A Cooper
Sacred Ring - Pagan Origins of British Folk Festivals, M. Howard
Season of Sorcery - On Becoming a Wisewoman, Poppy Palin
Seasonal Magic - Diary of a Village Witch, Paddy Slade
Secret Places of the Goddess, Philip Heselton
Secret Signs & Sigils, Nigel Pennick
Self Enlightenment, Mayan O'Brien
Spirits of the Air, Jaq D Hawkins
Spirits of the Earth, Jaq D Hawkins
Spirits of the Earth, Jaq D Hawkins
Taming the Wolf - Full Moon Meditations, Steve Hounsome
The Other Kingdoms Speak, Helena Hawley
Tree: Essence of Healing, Simon & Sue Lilly
Tree: Essence, Spirit & Teacher, Simon & Sue Lilly
Through the Veil, Peter Paddon
Torch and the Spear, Patrick Regan
Understanding Chaos Magic, Jaq D Hawkins
Vortex - The End of History, Mary Russell
Warriors at the Edge of Time, Jan Fry
Water Witches, Tony Steele
Way of the Magus, Michael Howard
Weaving a Web of Magic, Rhiannon Ryall
West Country Wicca, Rhiannon Ryall
Wildwitch - The Craft of the Natural Psychic, Poppy Palin

FREE detailed catalogue and
FREE 'Inspiration' magazine
Contact: Capall Bann Publishing, Freshfields, Chieveley, Berks, RG20 8TF

Capall Bann has moved from Berkshire and is now at:

**Auton Farm
Milverton
Somerset
TA4 1NE**

**Tel 01823 401528
www.capallbann.co.uk
enquiries@capallbann.co.uk**

A full detailed catalogue is available on request

Capall Bann has moved from Berkshire and is now at:

Auton Farm
Milverton
Somerset
TA4 1NE

Tel 01823 401528
www.capallbann.co.uk
enquiries@capallbann.co.uk

A full detailed catalogue is available on request